FROM AN IDEA TO
DISNEY

FROM AN IDEA TO
DISNEY

How Branding Made
Disney a Household Name

LOWEY BUNDY SICHOL

illustrated by C. S. JENNINGS

HOUGHTON MIFFLIN HARCOURT
Boston   New York

The text was set in ITC Galliard Std.

Library of Congress Cataloging-in-Publication Data
Names: Sichol, Lowey Bundy, author. Title: From an idea to Disney:
how branding made Disney a household name / by Lowey Bundy
Sichol. Description: New York, New York : Houghton Mifflin Harcourt
Publishing Company, [2018] | Series: From an idea to . . . ; 1 | Audience:
010–012. | Audience: 004–006. Identifiers: LCCN 2018032034 | ISBN
9781328453600 (paper over board) | ISBN 9781328453617 (paperback)
| ISBN 9781328530622 (E-Book) Subjects: LCSH: Walt Disney
Company—History—Juvenile literature. | Disney, Walt, 1901–1966—
Juvenile literature. | Branding (Marketing)—Juvenile literature. | LCGFT:
Biographies. Classification: LCC PN1999.W27 S53 2018 |
DDC 384/.80979494—dc23LC record available at
https://lccn.loc.gov/2018032034

Printed in the United States of America
DOC 10 9 8 7 6 5 4 3 2 1
4500745205

For Peyton, Carter, and Tucker, who believed in me and my idea that the world needs cool business books for kids. I love you more than anything.

Table of Contents

"I only hope that we never lose sight of one thing—that it was all started by a mouse."

—Walt Disney

What is the *business* story behind the Walt Disney Company?

When you think of Disney, you probably think of Mickey Mouse. That's not surprising, considering Mickey Mouse is the best-known cartoon character in the world. You probably can also name dozens, possibly hundreds, of other Disney characters. Perhaps you have been to Walt Disney World in Florida or Disneyland in California. Maybe you've watched the Disney Channel on TV, been on a Disney cruise, or seen a Disney on Broadway show.

Today, the Walt Disney Company is the biggest entertainment company in the world. But a long time ago, it was just an idea. An idea that two brothers, Walt and Roy Disney, had in 1923. This is the story of how a company that started with the idea of a cartoon mouse grew to be worth billions of dollars and employ more than 200,000 people worldwide.

1 Walt Disney's Childhood

Walter Elias Disney was born on December 5, 1901, in a rough neighborhood in Chicago, Illinois. When Walt was five, the Disney family moved to a forty-acre farm in Marceline, Missouri. Walt lived there with his parents, Elias and Flora Disney, and his four siblings, Herbert (twelve years older),

"When you're curious, you find lots of interesting things to do."
—Walt Disney

Raymond (ten years older), Roy (eight years older), and Ruth (two years younger).

Walt Disney had a very happy childhood and loved living on the farm. He enjoyed being surrounded by animals and nature but also was fascinated by trains and the way they transported people to exciting new places. Most likely, Walt's fascination with trains stemmed from his uncle Mike Martin, who was a steam locomotive engineer and traveled between Marceline and Fort Madison, Iowa.

As you can imagine, Walt was a very creative and curious boy. His favorite thing to do

was draw. Often, Walt drew the animals from the farm or the trains that steamed through his hometown of Marceline. Sometimes, Walt drew on things he wasn't supposed to, like on the side of his house with black tar or on his homework.

When Walt was nine, his father, Elias, became sick. Elias was not able to manage the farm anymore and decided to move his family to Kansas City. Walt was devastated. He hated to leave the farm, but Elias had no other choice.

At Walt's new school, he became the class clown, often performing funny skits in front of his classmates. Walt liked to make other kids laugh by drawing silly animal cartoons on the chalkboard. When Walt was fifteen, his family moved again. This time, they moved back to Chicago. Walt attended McKinley High School and took art classes in the evening at the Chicago Academy of Fine Arts. Walt did not like his high school, except for one thing—drawing cartoons for the school newspaper.

WALT'S FIRST JOBS

In 1919, at the age of eighteen, Walt moved to Kansas City, looking for work. By now, Walt had also started smoking cigarettes, a dangerous habit he continued throughout his life. Walt took a job at Pesmen-Rubin Commercial Art Studio, where he met Ub Iwerks, a man who would later become one of Walt's closest friends and colleagues.

After only one month, Walt and Ub were **laid off**, so they decided to start their own company, Iwerks-Disney Commercial Artists. Unfortunately, Iwerks-Disney did not make any money and shut down shortly after it opened. Halfheartedly, Walt took a job at the Kansas City Film

Laid off: Fired from a job, usually because the company cannot afford to keep the person.

Ad Company, making commercials based on animation. Although he did not want to make commercials, it was there that he learned all about animation. Fascinated with his new skill,

Walt decided to try to make his own animated cartoons.

Walt left the Kansas City Film Ad Company and started another company with Ub, called Laugh-O-gram Films. Laugh-O-gram Films created short, animated black-and-white cartoons that became popular in Kansas City but did not generate enough **revenue** to cover Walt's expenses. Eventually, Walt ran out of money and declared **bankruptcy.**

Revenue: The amount of money a company brings in for selling its products or services. Sometimes called "sales," "top line," or "gross income."

Bankruptcy: When a person or business does not have enough money to pay its debts.

2 Heading to Hollywood

During the 1920s, the only place people could watch cartoons was in movie theaters, usually just before the featured movie. All cartoons in those days came in black and white and had no sound. Artists drew each panel by hand, and most cartoons were produced in Hollywood, California, the same

"All our dreams can come true, if we have the courage to pursue them."
—Walt Disney

city where movies were made. Walt thought he had a better chance to succeed as a cartoonist if he lived and worked in Hollywood. So, at the age of twenty-two, Walt decided to move again.

With only forty dollars in his pocket, Walt left for Hollywood, excited and optimistic. His brother Roy was already living in California, and Walt thought, "I wanted Roy and I to be partners, that was all. I mean, we just wanted to be partners—*I* wanted it." The two brothers borrowed money from their parents, bought a new video camera, and opened the Disney Brothers Cartoon Studio in Hollywood in 1923.

Together, Walt and Roy were a good team. Walt drew the cartoons while Roy managed the business. Early on, Walt and Roy met with

a film distributor named Margaret Winkler. She presented them with a contract stating that she would pay the Disney Brothers Cartoon Studio for twelve films—$1,500 for each of the first six films and $1,800 for each of the next six films. In addition, Margaret Winkler would receive the **intellectual property rights** to everything the Disney Brothers Cartoon Studio

> **Intellectual property rights:** Ownership of a creative work or invention.

created. Although it wasn't a great deal, it was work, and Walt signed the contract.

Soon thereafter, Walt and Roy Disney hired two women to help with the increased workload. Walt would draw the outlines of the cartoon characters, and the two women would fill in—or ink—them.

Walt fell in love with one of these women, Lillian Bounds. On July 13, 1925, Walt and Lillian got married. In 1926, the Disney Brothers Cartoon Studio changed its name to

Walt Disney Studios to reflect Walt's talent and vision.

OSWALD THE LUCKY RABBIT

Walt Disney Studios had some success early on with one of their cartoon characters named Oswald the Lucky Rabbit. Meanwhile, Margaret Winkler married a man named Charles Mintz, who took over her business. Charles Mintz, however, had a sneaky plan up his sleeve. He wanted to get rid of Walt and Roy and take over Walt Disney Studios!

Charles Mintz approached Walt with a second contract. It stated that Walt Disney

AGREEMENT

GIVE OSWALD THE LUCKY RABBIT TO CHARLES MINTZ

Walt Disney

Studios would produce twenty-six animated short cartoons featuring Oswald the Lucky Rabbit, but Charles Mintz would pay them only $1,500 for each film. This was even less money than the first contract and, again, gave Charles Mintz the intellectual property rights to everything Walt Disney Studios created. But Walt needed the work, so he signed the contract and hired several more artists and animators, including Walt's good friend Ub Iwerks.

With the new films, Oswald the Lucky

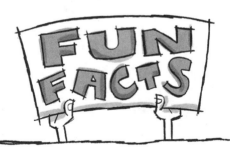

In 2006, the Walt Disney Company bought the rights to Oswald the Lucky Rabbit from NBC/Universal. Soon thereafter, Oswald made a cameo appearance in the movies *Big Hero 6* and *Zootopia*.

Rabbit became very popular among children and adults. However, Charles Mintz's plan to take over Walt Disney Studios soon went into effect. First, Charles Mintz signed a new three-year agreement with Universal Studios to create more Oswald the Lucky Rabbit cartoons. Then, without Walt and Roy knowing, Charles Mintz approached the artists and animators at Walt Disney Studios and hired them away—all of them except Ub Iwerks!

Charles Mintz now owned Oswald the Lucky Rabbit and employed most of Walt's employees. Walt was furious! He and Lillian took a train ride to New York City to try to negotiate a new deal, but Charles Mintz only offered Walt even less money and now wanted full control of Walt Disney Studios. Walt refused the deal and walked away.

AN IDEA . . .

Angry and frustrated, Walt and Lillian Disney headed back home on a train from Manhattan to Hollywood. It was then that an idea popped into Walt's head . . .

Walt's idea was a cartoon mouse.

Walt quickly sketched the mouse on a

pad of paper. The mouse had round black ears, a white face, a big smile, and a long tail. Walt showed it to Lillian and announced the mouse's name . . . Mortimer Mouse!

"Mortimer Mouse?" Lillian questioned. She did not like the sound of the name Mortimer. Several days later, Lillian suggested a differ-ent name. Lillian Disney suggested Mickey Mouse.

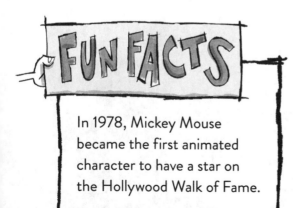

3 Mickey Mouse and Snow White

Walt returned home and created the first two Mickey Mouse cartoons. Unfortunately, they flopped. No movie theaters wanted to buy them. Walt knew he had to create something new and spectacular to save Mickey Mouse from being a failure. Walt had to add **innovation** to his work. So he did something that

"The way to get started is to quit talking and begin doing."
—Walt Disney

had never been done before. Walt added *sound* to a cartoon for the first time ever.

> **Innovation:** A revolutionary new way of doing something. This could be a new idea, a new method, or a new product.

On November 18, 1928, Walt Disney Studios released a cartoon called *Steamboat Willie*. It featured Mickey Mouse as the captain of a ship, whistling and singing along to synchronized music. Audiences were amazed!

Over the next few years, demand for Mickey Mouse cartoons exploded, and Walt hired more employees to keep up. They introduced new characters like Minnie Mouse, Donald Duck, Pluto, and Goofy. They launched the Mickey Mouse Club and ran a Mickey Mouse comic strip in newspapers. In 1929, Walt Disney Studios changed its name to Walt Disney Productions. In 1932, Walt Disney Productions innovated its cartoons even further and released a cartoon in color for the first time. Walt now realized that innovation was the key to his company's success!

Mickey Mouse and his friends became very popular. Children found the color and sound

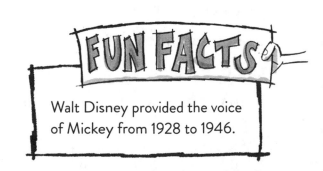

FUN FACTS

Walt Disney provided the voice of Mickey from 1928 to 1946.

of Walt Disney's cartoons to be a truly magical experience. They stood in long lines just for the chance to watch a Disney cartoon at their local movie theater.

Intrigued by the popularity of his short cartoons, Walt had an idea about a new way to innovate them. He believed that if children could sit and watch Mickey Mouse cartoons for hours at a time, then they would really enjoy a *full-length* cartoon movie. Many people disagreed. There had never been a full-length cartoon movie before, and the idea seemed crazy. Once again, Walt was determined and worked tirelessly to make his vision a reality.

SNOW WHITE AND THE SEVEN DWARFS

Walt Disney Productions based its first full-length movie on the fairy tale "Snow White and the Seven Dwarfs," written by the Brothers Grimm. Walt thought the fairy tale had a nice balance of excitement and humor.

The movie, *Snow White and the Seven Dwarfs*, took three years to complete and cost $1.5 million—

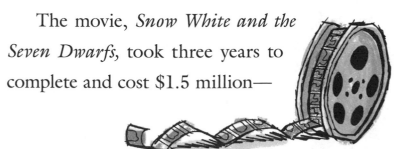

> **The Great Depression:** This was a period of time when the world's economy collapsed. Millions of people lost their jobs, and many lost their homes, possessions, and even all their money. People struggled to afford necessities like food, clothes, and shelter. Many stood in line for hours just for a free loaf of bread.

an enormous amount of money, especially during **the Great Depression**. To come up with $1.5 million, Walt had to take out a **mortgage**.

On December 21, 1937, *Snow White and the Seven Dwarfs* was shown to the public for the first time. Thanks to the thrilling and often scary story line, the utter beauty of the artwork, and Walt Disney Productions' new multiplane camera, which created a three-dimensional effect on film, *Snow White and*

Mortgage: A way to borrow money from a bank using one's house or land as collateral. That means the bank loans a person money and the person pays the bank back in monthly installments over a long period of time. The bank makes money because it also charges interest, which is an additional type of payment. If the person does not pay the bank back in time, the bank can take ownership of the person's house or land.

the Seven Dwarfs was a smashing success, earning $8 million during its initial release. That's $137 million today! In addition to bringing in millions of dollars to the company, the film won an Honorary Oscar in 1939 for creating

After adjusting for inflation, *Snow White and the Seven Dwarfs* has earned a whopping $418.2 million over its lifetime. This puts it among the top American film moneymakers of all time.

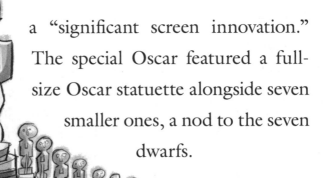

a "significant screen innovation." The special Oscar featured a full-size Oscar statuette alongside seven smaller ones, a nod to the seven dwarfs.

FUN FACTS

Walt Disney received many Academy Awards. He won four Honorary Awards and twenty-two competitive awards for a total of twenty-six Academy Awards, the most by any one individual. His films were nominated fifty-nine times, also the most for any one individual. And he holds the record for receiving the most Academy Awards in one year—in 1954, he won four Oscars and was nominated six times.

How Disney Went Public

4

With the money made from *Snow White and the Seven Dwarfs,* Walt Disney Productions created and released four more feature-length films in the following years: *Fantasia* and *Pinocchio* in 1940, *Dumbo* in 1941, and *Bambi* in 1942. None of the films performed as well financially as *Snow White and the*

"Do a good job. You don't have to worry about the money; it will take care of itself. Just do your best work—then try to trump it." —Walt Disney

Seven Dwarfs, so Walt needed to consider new ways to raise money.

When a company wants to raise money, it often considers **going public** (see page 28). Walt wasn't quite ready to take Walt Disney Productions public. First, he wanted to try to increase the value of the company.

Walt Disney Productions released another wave of animated movies: *Cinderella* in 1950, *Alice in Wonderland* in 1951, and *Peter Pan* in 1953. It also released live-action films, including *Treasure Island* in 1950 and *20,000 Leagues Under the Sea* in 1954. In 1955, the Disneyland amusement park opened to the

FUN FACTS

If you had invested $1,000 in Disney's initial public offering back in 1957, it would be worth $3,266,000 in 2015.

public (more on this in the next chapter). By 1957, the value of Walt Disney Productions had significantly increased. Walt decided it was finally time to go public.

Walt Disney Productions went public on November 12, 1957.

On the first day of trading, the company's stock price was sold at $13.88 per share. In April 1959, Walt Disney Productions' stock price had increased to $52.50 per share.

WHAT DOES "GOING PUBLIC" MEAN?

Every new company starts off as a **private company** or a **privately held company**. That means the founders who started the business own the entire company and run it the way they want. The founders make all the key decisions for the company. These decisions are private information and not shared with the public.

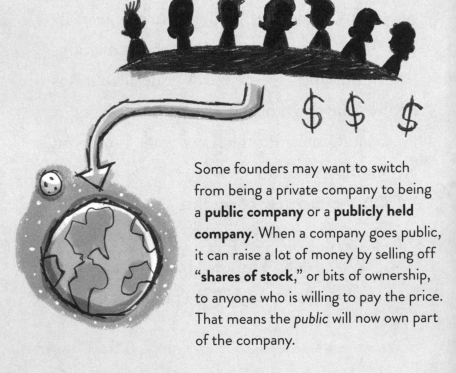

Some founders may want to switch from being a private company to being a **public company** or a **publicly held company**. When a company goes public, it can raise a lot of money by selling off **"shares of stock,"** or bits of ownership, to anyone who is willing to pay the price. That means the *public* will now own part of the company.

One way to think about going public is to think of a company as a building. Each brick of the building is like a share of stock.

1.50 MILLION BRICKS →

When a company is private, the founders and private investors own all the bricks of the building (or the entire company).

When a company goes public, the founders and private investors sell off a specific number of bricks (or shares of stock) for money—so other people now have a chance to own some of the company. The people who buy and own these shares are called **shareholders**. The price for each brick (or share) can range from a few cents to thousands of dollars based on how well the company is doing. The more each brick (or share) is worth, the more valuable the building (or company) is worth.

WHY DO STOCK PRICES GO UP AND DOWN?

A company can have a high or low stock price for many reasons. A high stock price usually means the company's products are selling well, it is making lots of money, and good leaders are in place. Most people want to own shares of stock in a company that is doing very well and is expected to grow bigger, so the price goes up.

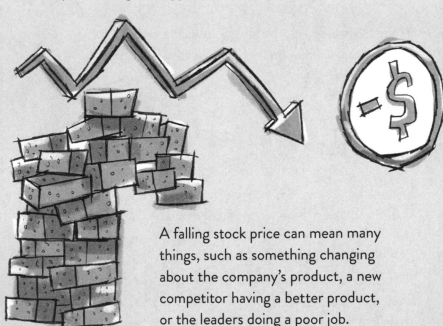

A falling stock price can mean many things, such as something changing about the company's product, a new competitor having a better product, or the leaders doing a poor job.

The more shares someone holds in one company, the more ownership he or she possesses. For example, after Disney bought Pixar in 2006, Steve Jobs, the founder of Apple and a leader at Pixar, owned 138 million shares of Disney stock. That meant Steve Jobs owned a 7.4 percent slice of the Disney pie.

WHY DO COMPANIES GO PUBLIC?

The main reason companies decide to go public is to raise money. They can use this money to expand into new areas, develop new products, acquire new companies, hire more people, or pay off debt.

That might sound like a good deal, but there are challenges, too. When a company goes public, there are lots (sometimes tens of millions) of people who now own a little bit of the company. In addition, a public company must follow the rules and regulations set by a department of the U.S. government called the Securities and Exchange Commission (SEC).

The job of the SEC is to protect investors from any sort of dishonest business. The SEC makes and enforces strict rules and regulations that all public companies must follow.

Not every company believes going public is worth the effort of having to follow these rules and regulations or sharing its company information with the public.

5 The Magic of Disneyland

Walt was the father of two girls, Diane Marie and Sharon Mae, and believed nothing was more important than family. He drove his girls to school every single day, enjoyed Daddy's Day on the weekends, and liked to visit places that they could enjoy together as a family. However, Walt realized few places like

"You can design and create, and build the most wonderful place in the world. But it takes people to make the dream a reality."
—Walt Disney

that existed. Amusement parks, circuses, and carnivals were often dirty and not focused on the needs of families.

Then Walt had an idea . . . He dreamed of creating a family destination where children and adults could have fun together and experience the magic of Disney in person. He also wanted it to be *more* than just an amusement park. It had to be impeccably clean and well laid out. It had to have a variety of fun rides and attractions. It had to have a train that encircled the entire park, plus a village, and places to buy food and Disney **merchandise.** He would call it Disneyland.

> **Merchandise:** Items for sale. At Disneyland, that would include Mickey Mouse–shaped ears, candy, and balloons, along with clothing and toys.

It was the early 1950s, before the company

went public, and Walt believed his vision of Disneyland would increase the value of his company. But Walt also knew Disneyland was going to be very expensive to build. While the company had earned some money from its movies, it needed much more to make Disneyland come to life. Determined as ever, Walt turned to television.

In the 1950s, television was the latest and greatest technology. Families usually owned only one television set, and all family members would gather around it each night to watch a show together.

Walt Disney Productions created a Disney television series called *Walt Disney Presents*, and later, *Walt Disney's Wonderful World of Color*, which aired Sunday nights on ABC. Each week, the show would announce its theme— Fantasyland, Tomorrowland, Frontierland, or Adventureland. If it were a Fantasyland theme, it would usually air cartoons or *The Mickey*

Mouse Club. Tomorrowland brought science and technology themes, such as "Our Friend the Atom." Frontierland's most popular heroes were Davy Crockett and Zorro, while Adventureland featured pirates and explorers. Walt himself was the show's host, and he soon became a familiar face to the children and families who watched the show each week. Disney's television series quickly became popular and made so much money that Walt was ready to start the development of Disneyland.

In 1954, Walt pulled together a team

FUN FACTS

Walt Disney liked to disguise himself in a floppy hat and sunglasses and walk around Disneyland during the day. Sometimes children would recognize him.

of designers and engineers and called them
"Imagineers." He sent his Imagineers to every
single amusement park in the United States.
Walt wanted his Imagineers to understand
every aspect about what made amusement
parks fun and successful and, perhaps more
importantly, what caused problems or made
customers unhappy.

Walt wasn't just interested in the big take-aways; he wanted his team to think about every single detail. Walt believed that solutions for small problems—like how to keep birds away from food areas and how to keep the walkways always clean—were just as important as big concepts, like how to make a roller coaster thrilling and safe. Walt wanted Disneyland to be the most magical place on earth.

Before Disneyland could open to the public, the company had to hire and train its employees. Walt renamed his employees "cast members" and considered them a critical

> **Customer service:** The way a company treats its customers or visitors.

part to the success of Disneyland. They had to be friendly, polite, and helpful, plus they had to work together to run the rides and keep Disneyland spotless. In short, Walt wanted Disneyland to have the best **customer service** in the world. As part of the training, cast members were required to attend Disney University, a training facility that taught everything from how to work each ride to how to help a lost child.

Disneyland opened in July 1955. The opening ceremonies were shown live on ABC and viewed by tens of millions of people all over the country. Disneyland was everything Walt dreamed it would be. It was a destination where families could experience the magic of Disney in real life. There was a train that encircled the park and brought visitors to different areas, including Fantasyland, with fairy-tale characters and a castle; Adventureland, with an adventure theme; Frontierland, featuring cowboys and the Wild West; Tomorrowland, with its futuristic theme; and a Main Street that was modeled after Walt's childhood hometown of

Many of the original rides at Disneyland still exist today, including Disneyland Railroad, Mad Tea Party, Peter Pan's Flight, King Arthur Carousel, Mr. Toad's Wild Ride, Storybook Land Canal Boats, Snow White's Adventures, Autopia, Mark Twain Riverboat, Dumbo the Flying Elephant, and Jungle Cruise.

Marceline, Missouri. Main Street was filled with shops, restaurants, and life-size Disney characters in full costume, from Mickey Mouse and Donald Duck to Peter Pan and Cinderella. By the end of its first month, Disneyland had more than twenty thousand visitors a day.

WALT'S LAST YEARS

After Disneyland launched, Walt spent most of his time developing two new ideas. One was for a full-length movie that combined live action and animation. The movie was called *Mary Poppins* and was lightly based on the Mary Poppins book series by P. L. Travers. *Mary Poppins* became a box office smash in 1964, earning thirteen Oscar nominations, including Disney's first Best Picture nomination. Walt's other big idea was to create a destination unlike any place in the world. In 1965,

Walt Disney would visit Disneyland after everyone had left and drive a mini fire engine through the streets.

Walt laid out his vision for Disney World (now called Walt Disney World) in Orlando, Florida. It would include the Magic Kingdom, a larger version of Disneyland, as well as golf courses, resorts, and Epcot, which stood for Experimental Prototype Community of Tomorrow.

Unfortunately, Walt never saw his dream of Walt Disney World come to life. A longtime cigarette smoker, Walt became very sick with lung cancer in 1966. He died on December 15, 1966, at the age of sixty-five.

6 The Disney Brand

When Walt died in 1966, he was considered one of the most famous people in the world. Also, Walt Disney was now one of the most recognized brands in the world. A brand is the personality or image that is created around a company or name. It builds over time from the experiences people have with a

"I am interested in entertaining people, in bringing pleasure, particularly laughter, to others." —Walt Disney

company's products and services, and from the interactions they have with its employees.

There are strong brands and weak brands. A strong brand means people like the brand, prefer it over the competition, and are very loyal to it. A strong brand also adds value to a company and helps increase the price of a company's stock. Once a company has a strong brand, it can expand more easily into new areas and customers will follow because they trust the brand to continue giving them good products or experiences. For Disney, it expanded from cartoons to movies to television to theme parks. As it expanded, Disney's customers trusted that Disney would always deliver on its brand promise—high-quality, fun entertainment for the whole family.

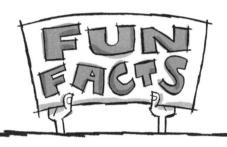

Today, more than seventy thousand cast members work at Walt Disney World Resort, making it the largest single-site employer in the United States. All cast members are still required to attend Disney University for several days before beginning their onsite training. The first class is called Traditions, where new cast members are welcomed into the Disney family and taught about the legacy and history of the Disney brand.

It's a
Hard Time
After All

7

After Walt's death, Roy Disney took over as **CEO**. He fulfilled his brother's dream of opening the twenty-four-thousand-acre Walt Disney World theme park in Orlando, Florida, in 1971. Unfortunately, Roy died later that same year.

Walt Disney Productions now had a

"You may not realize it when it happens, but a kick in the teeth may be the best thing in the world for you."

—Walt Disney

problem: both Disney brothers had died within five years of each other. These two men were not only the founders of Walt Disney Productions, but also the two people with the vision and drive to make the cartoons, movies, characters, and theme parks a reality. Now that they were gone, who would run the company?

For many years, the company didn't have an answer. From 1971 to 1984, Walt Disney Productions had three different CEOs. However, none of them had the vision,

FUN FACTS

In an effort to keep Disneyland and Walt Disney World clean, the theme parks do not sell gum anywhere.

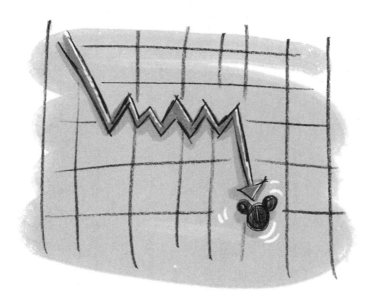

innovation, or leadership skills to run Walt Disney Productions and maintain the Disney brand. The company struggled. Fewer people visited Disneyland and Walt Disney World, television ratings dropped, and no new animated movies were made. Sales plummeted, and Disney's stock price fell. Disney weakened financially and strategically. Without the vision of Walt and Roy Disney, the company seemed to have lost its magic, and people no longer felt a strong connection to the Disney brand.

NEW LEADERSHIP

In 1984, Walt Disney Productions hired a man named Michael Eisner as its new CEO. Prior to Disney, Michael Eisner had been president and CEO of Paramount Pictures, a movie studio that produced many well-known movies such as *Saturday Night Fever*, *Grease*, and *Star Trek*.

Michael Eisner was a creative person and full of ideas. Walking into Walt Disney Productions, he had a plan. Michael Eisner believed that for the company to get back on track, it needed to do three things. First, Disney had to reconnect with children and families, its core

audience. Second, Disney had to create excitement around what Disney does best—making
animated movies and creating high-quality
theme parks. Third, Disney had to reach more
people—many more people.

8

One Hundred and One Improvements

In 1989, the newly renamed Walt Disney Company released a movie that seemed more like a Broadway show than a cartoon. Based on a Hans Christian Andersen fairy tale, it was about a teenage mermaid longing to become a human and featured Oscar-winning songs, singing, dancing, and a beautiful storyline

"It's kind of fun to do the impossible." —Walt Disney

with a happy ending. The movie was *The Little Mermaid*. *The Little Mermaid* sparked an era known as the "Disney Renaissance."

Renaissance: Rebirth or reawakening.

THE DISNEY RENAISSANCE

The Disney Renaissance occurred between the late 1980s and the early 2000s. It was a period of time when the Walt Disney Company surged back to life, restoring trust and loyalty in people's minds. Michael Eisner accomplished this by following his three strategies.

First, Disney went back to doing what it did best—making animated movies. Throughout the 1990s and early 2000s, Disney released many groundbreaking animated films, each one filled with high-quality animation, award-winning music, and humor that was adored by both kids and adults. Movies like *Beauty and the Beast* (1991), *Aladdin* (1992),

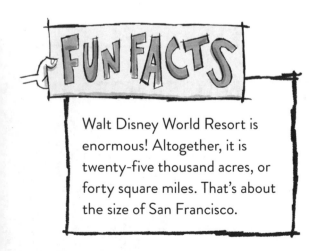

FUN FACTS

Walt Disney World Resort is enormous! Altogether, it is twenty-five thousand acres, or forty square miles. That's about the size of San Francisco.

The Lion King (1994), *Toy Story* (with Pixar, 1995), *Mulan* (1998), *Monsters, Inc.* (2001), *Lilo & Stitch* (2002), *Finding Nemo* (2003), *The Incredibles* (2004), and *Cars* (2006) were all box office hits and captured the hearts of

children and adults alike. Many of these movies won Oscar awards, too.

Second, the Walt Disney Company focused on television. It changed the name of its television series to *The Disney Sunday Movie* and featured classic Disney films such as *The Love Bug, Mary Poppins,* and *The Parent Trap.* It was an effective way to reach a whole new generation of children. Families would gather together on

Sunday nights and watch classic movies from when the parents were young, just as their parents had watched *Walt Disney Presents* on Sunday nights when they were young.

Third, as home movies grew in popularity, the Walt Disney Company released classic movies like *Cinderella* and *Lady and the Tramp* and new movies on videotapes and DVDs at

Since opening, Walt Disney World has been closed only five times, all due to hurricanes. Walt Disney World closed on September 15, 1999, for Hurricane Floyd; September 4–5, 2004, for Hurricane Frances; September 26, 2004, for Hurricane Jeanne; October 7, 2016, for Hurricane Matthew; and September 9–11, 2017, for Hurricane Irma. After the terrorist attacks in New York City on September 11, 2001, Walt Disney World was evacuated in less than thirty minutes.

affordable prices. Now families could bring the magical world of Disney right into their living rooms and watch Disney movies as often as they wished.

9 Michael Eisner's Wild Ride

Michael Eisner's plan worked. Sales at Disney skyrocketed as people embraced a whole new wave of Disney movies and characters. Michael Eisner felt it was the perfect time to expand the Disney brand into new areas and locations in hopes of gaining even more customers.

"We keep moving forward, opening new doors, and doing new things, because we're curious and curiosity keeps leading us down new paths." —Walt Disney

The Walt Disney Company opened seven new Disney theme parks, including two overseas—Tokyo Disneyland and Euro Disney Resort (now called Disneyland Paris). It renovated old attractions at Disneyland, which were thirty-five years old at the time, and opened new attractions, such as Captain EO and Star Tours, which targeted older children and teenagers. At Walt Disney World, the company expanded with several new theme parks, including Hollywood Studios and Animal Kingdom; at Disneyland, it opened Disney California Adventure. It was an exciting time for Disney theme parks. Visitors came from all over the world, and sales grew.

The Walt Disney Company expanded in television, too. During the 1990s, the Walt Disney Company **acquired** ABC and ten cable channels, including the popular

Acquire: To purchase another company.

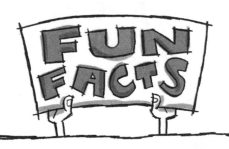

Mickey Mouse has more than 130 different outfits, ranging from a scuba suit to a tuxedo. Minnie Mouse has more than 100 outfits, ranging from a cheerleader uniform to evening gowns.

sports channel ESPN. It created the Disney Channel, which aired Disney cartoons and movies twenty-four hours a day, seven days a week, and became a favorite channel of many children. Disney was now one of the biggest television companies in the world.

The Walt Disney Company even brought the magic of Disney to the prestige of New York City's Broadway theaters. Disney on Broadway opened *Beauty and the Beast* in 1994 and *The Lion King* in 1997. Both theatrical productions were very successful and led to future Broadway shows like *Mary Poppins* and *Aladdin*.

The Walt Disney Company continued to expand its brand into new areas. Here are some examples of Disney's brand extensions during Michael Eisner's reign as CEO:

STORES—The company opened Disney Stores all over the country, which sold merchandise like toys, costumes, and clothing.

CRUISE SHIPS—Disney Cruise Lines set sail, entertaining families throughout the Caribbean.

 BOOKS AND MAGAZINES—The Disney Publishing Group produced *Disney Magazine* and published books based on Disney stories and Disney characters.

REAL ESTATE—Disney Real Estate sold vacation homes near Walt Disney World Resort.

SPORTS—The Walt Disney Company even entered the world of professional sports. In 1993, Disney launched a National Hockey League (NHL) expansion team called the Mighty Ducks of Anaheim. In 1997, Disney purchased and took control of a Major League Baseball (MLB) team, the Anaheim Angels.

During the time Michael Eisner led the Walt Disney Company, Disney exploded in growth on many levels. Sales grew from $1.5 billion a year to more than $80 billion a year. Stocks surged, sending Disney's **market value**

> **Market value:** A calculation used to determine the value of a company. Market value equals current share price multiplied by the number of outstanding shares.

from $2 billion to $67 billion. And the number of cast members grew from 28,000 to 129,000!

Disney, it seemed, was everywhere. But now the company had a different problem . . .

10 The Rescuers

Some Disney cast members, fans, and **executives**, including Walt's nephew,

Executive: An individual who holds an important leadership position within a company and helps make major decisions.

Roy E. Disney, were angry. They thought Michael Eisner had expanded the Disney brand *too* much and was *too* focused on

"When you believe in a thing, believe in it all the way, implicitly and unquestionably." —Walt Disney

> **Dilute:** To weaken. When a company dilutes its brand, it expands into too many areas and loses focus on what is special about its brand.

making a profit at any expense. They thought Michael Eisner had **diluted** the Disney brand. Instead, Roy E. Disney and his supporters wanted to preserve the heritage and magic around the Disney name and brand. On top of that, Michael Eisner was known for being a challenging man to work for and **employee morale** seemed low.

> **Employee morale:** Overall job satisfaction and feelings employees have in the workplace. High employee morale means people are happy and want to work hard at their jobs. Low employee morale means people are unhappy, frustrated, and dissatisfied with their jobs.

Roy E. Disney and his supporters wanted change, starting with Michael Eisner. They wanted Michael Eisner to leave the Walt Disney Company. But because he was the CEO, the only way to fire Michael Eisner was to encourage the **board of directors** and stock

> **Board of directors:** A group of individuals that are elected as representatives of the stockholders. They help make major company decisions, like hiring and firing a CEO. Every public company must have a board of directors. Some private companies have them, too.

owners to vote him out. Soon, a group called Save Disney was established to do just that. In 2004, the board of directors voted that Michael Eisner step down as chairman of the board. Later, under pressure from the board, he resigned as CEO.

Despite the abrupt ending to Michael Eisner's career at Disney, he would be remembered as being a very smart, very successful

businessman. During the twenty years he had been CEO, the Walt Disney Company had grown from a struggling entertainment company into a major media corporation.

BOB IGER BECOMES THE NEXT CEO

Disney announced its next CEO—a man named Bob Iger. Bob Iger had been in the entertainment business since 1974. He started his career at ABC as a weatherman in Ithaca,

New York, and worked his way up over the years, eventually becoming president and chief operating officer of the Walt Disney Company in 2000.

One of Bob Iger's biggest challenges was to keep Disney fresh and exciting while staying true to its heritage and traditions. Bob Iger explained, "When you deal with a company that has a great legacy, you deal with decisions and conflicts that arise from the clash of heritage versus innovation versus relevance. I'm a big believer in respect for heritage, but I'm also a big believer in the need to innovate and the need to balance that respect for heritage with a need to

Ever wonder what the tallest attractions at Walt Disney World are?

1. Expedition Everest at Disney's Animal Kingdom—200 feet

2. The Twilight Zone Tower of Terror at Disney's Hollywood Studios—199 feet

3. Magic Kingdom's Cinderella Castle—189 feet

4. Spaceship Earth at Epcot—183 feet

5. Space Mountain at Magic Kingdom—180 feet

6. The Tree of Life at Disney's Animal Kingdom—145 feet

be relevant." That meant that when he became CEO of Disney, Bob Iger had to balance keeping Disney true to its beloved history while growing the company with new ideas.

DISNEY'S HEART AND SOUL

Bob Iger understood that Disney's heart and soul belong in its movies and theme parks. He believed a good way to stay true to Disney's heritage was to get rid of the businesses that were not related to Disney's heart and soul. So Bob Iger immediately started to divest, or sell off, parts of the company. He sold Disney Stores to a company called the Children's Place and stopped the publication of *Disney Magazine*. Next, he sold the NHL team, Mighty Ducks of Anaheim, which was later renamed Anaheim Ducks, and the MLB team, the Anaheim Angels, which was later renamed the Los Angeles Angels.

On the flip side, Bob Iger needed to grow sales, so he planned to acquire film studios that complemented the Disney brand. Over the next decade, Bob Iger led several important acquisitions. In 2004, the Walt Disney Company acquired Jim Henson's Muppets after years of partnering together. Disney now owned the rights to well-known characters like Kermit the Frog, Miss Piggy, and Fozzy Bear. In 2006, Disney acquired the animation movie studio Pixar. In the past, Disney and

Pixar had worked together on making movies such as *Toy Story, Finding Nemo,* and *Monsters, Inc.* Because of their previous partnerships together, Bob Iger believed Pixar would be a good fit with the Disney brand. And he was right! Together, Disney/Pixar released several blockbuster movies, including *Up, Brave, Inside Out,* and *Finding Dory.* In 2009, Disney acquired Marvel, the studio that created many superhero characters, including Spider-Man,

Iron Man, and the Hulk. With these new characters, Disney released movies such as *Thor, The Avengers,* and *Guardians of the Galaxy.* In

2012, Disney acquired Lucasfilm, the company that created *Star Wars.* Bob Iger explained, "[*Star Wars*] is one of the great entertainment properties of all time, one of the best branded and one of the most valuable, and it's just fantastic for us to have the opportunity to both buy it, run it, and grow it."

FROZEN HELPS DISNEY "LET IT GO"

Disney released an animated movie in 2013 that shattered everyone's expectations. *Frozen,* a film about two sisters—one who was born with magical powers she couldn't control and one who becomes a hero with a selfless act of sacrifice—broke just about every record for an animated movie. It seemed everyone, from toddlers to adults, found something to relate to in *Frozen* and its songs. *Frozen* earned more than $1.2 billion at the box office, the most by any animated movie in history. *Frozen* won Academy Awards and Golden Globes. The *Frozen* soundtrack sold millions of copies. The *Frozen* DVD became Amazon's best-selling

FUN FACTS

Frozen was based on the Hans Christian Andersen fairy tale called "The Snow Queen." Say the names of the main Frozen characters quickly: Hans—Kristoff—Anna—Sven. It sounds like Hans Christian Andersen!

children's film of all time and the show was adapted for Broadway. *Frozen* not only lifted Disney to yet another level of success, but also confirmed that Bob Iger was, indeed, the right person for the job.

One Hundred Years Later

Walt Disney was a person who began with an idea, then followed his passion. He created cartoons that were unique, exciting, risky, and fun. Walt continued to challenge himself and take risks with innovative ideas. He added sound and color to cartoons, even when he was on the verge of losing everything. He

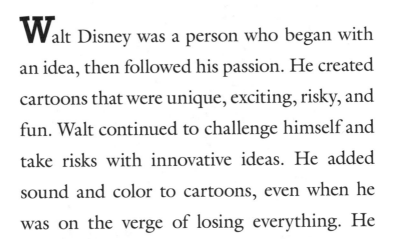

"If you can dream it, you can do it."
—Walt Disney

created the first full-length cartoon movie, *Snow White and the Seven Dwarfs,* even when others thought it would fail. He created the best, cleanest, most magical family amusement park in the world, Disneyland, even when others doubted him. Just before he died, Walt laid out his vision to keep the Walt Disney Company moving forward with the development of Walt Disney World and Epcot. Walt Disney created the Disney brand.

A subsequent CEO, Michael Eisner, grew the Walt Disney Company into a multibillion-dollar company by expanding the Disney

Disney sells more than seventy-five million Cokes and thirteen million bottles of water each year at Walt Disney World Resort.

brand into new areas like publishing, theater, retail, cruise lines, and real estate, as well as new locations like Europe and Asia. Most recently, CEO Bob Iger brought the Walt Disney Company back to its heart and soul by divesting parts of the company that didn't fit with the Disney brand, such as sports teams and clothing. Bob Iger has grown the company

FUN FACTS

When Disney's Magic Kingdom first opened in 1971, adult admission cost $3.50.

by acquiring companies that complement the Disney brand and creating new movies, characters, and theme park experiences.

It has been almost one hundred years since Walt and Roy Disney started the Walt Disney Company in 1923, and it is bigger and better than ever before. The company estimates that, altogether, its customers spend thirteen

billion hours each year interacting with the Disney brand. People around the world spend ten billion hours watching programs on the Disney Channel, eight hundred million hours at Disney's resorts and theme parks, and more than one billion hours watching Disney movies—at home, in the theater, or on their mobile devices. Today, Disney is one of the most powerful brands in the world.

EVERYTHING MATTERS

Despite being so big, the Disney brand continues to feel small and special. Why? Because to the Walt Disney Company, *everything* is important—from big ideas, like buying the *Star Wars* franchise, to the smallest detail, like not selling bubblegum at its theme parks (so visitors will never step on chewed-up gum). Walt Disney himself had an eye for detail and believed in providing an experience, not a single product. Walt thought products could be easily copied by others, while a magical experience was unique and stayed with a person forever.

Take, for example, Walt Disney World Resort. The most magical place on earth is also an example of how Disney considers the impact of everything associated with its brand. As visitors enter the front gates of each theme park, cast members greet them by waving big Mickey Mouse hands and handing out maps, buttons, and stickers, while Disney characters create unique photo opportunities. It's a friendly way to be greeted, but there are additional reasons for their actions. Cast members are purposely distracting the huge crowds so everyone doesn't rush off to the same big attractions. Meanwhile, the stores on Main Street pump out sweet smells of candy and cinnamon to keep the mood fun and exciting. The sugary scents also trigger children to ask their parents to buy treats for them. Consider the thousands of pounds of garbage produced at Walt Disney World every day; yet it's hard to find a piece of trash anywhere. Not only do cast members make sure every speck of garbage is picked up, but also, the bottoms of the trash cans connect to underground tunnels that suck the garbage away without being noticed. That way, guests never see a garbage truck or an overflowing garbage can during their visit. Even the street sweepers are trained by Disney's animators to take their simple broom and bucket of water and quietly paint a Goofy or Mickey Mouse in water on the pavement while guests wait in line. It's a moment of magic that lasts just a few seconds before it evaporates in the hot sun.

The part of Walt Disney World's Magic Kingdom that you see is built on the second level of the resort! Below where you walk lies an entire community filled with restaurants, kitchens, restrooms, changing rooms, hair salons, makeup studios, secret staircases, even bicycles and golf carts to take cast members from one place to another.

Just like those who questioned Walt Disney making a full-length animated film, some wonder why a company would go to the trouble of hiring someone to draw an image in water that would disappear in a matter of seconds. The answer? Because it's a magical experience. It's all part of the Disney brand.

Today, the Walt Disney Company truly runs by Walt Disney's words:

"Whatever you do, do it well. Do it so well that when people see you do it they will want to come back and see you do it again and they will want to bring others and show them how well you do what you do."

—Walt Disney

TIMELINE OF THE WALT DISNEY COMPANY

1901 • Walt Disney is born on December 5 in Chicago, Illinois.

1922 • Walt Disney and Ub Iwerks start a company called Laugh-O-gram Films, which makes cartoons. The business doesn't sell enough cartoons to cover the costs and declares bankruptcy.

1923 • Walt moves to Hollywood and partners with his older brother Roy to start the Disney Brothers Cartoon Studio.

1926 • The name Disney Brothers Cartoon Studio changes to Walt Disney Studios to reflect Walt's vision.

1928 • Walt creates Mickey Mouse. Walt Disney Studios releases *Steamboat Willie*, the first cartoon with sound.

1929 • Walt Disney Studios changes its name to Walt Disney Productions. New characters like Minnie Mouse and Goofy are introduced.

1932 • Walt Disney Productions releases the first cartoons in color.

1937 • Walt Disney Productions releases *Snow White and the Seven Dwarfs,* the first animated full-length movie.

1940–1953 • Disney releases several new animated feature films, including *Fantasia* (1940), *Pinocchio* (1940), *Dumbo* (1941), *Bambi* (1942), *Cinderella* (1950), and *Peter Pan* (1953). These movies help increase the value of the company.

1954 • Disney's first television show airs.

1955 • Disneyland opens.

1957 • Walt Disney Productions goes public on November 12.

1964 • Disney releases *Mary Poppins,* its biggest movie of the 1960s and the first movie to combine live action and animation. It is nominated for thirteen Oscars and wins five.

1966 • Walt Disney dies of lung cancer at the age of sixty-five.

1971 • Walt Disney World opens. Roy Disney dies later that same year.

1971–1983 • Walt Disney Productions stumbles. Sales drop and stocks fall as the company searches for the right CEO.

1984 • Michael Eisner is hired as CEO. Disney

stock price lingers around one dollar per share. Disney releases its first movie on VHS cassettes.

1986 • Walt Disney Productions changes its name to the Walt Disney Company.

1989 • *The Little Mermaid* is released, launching a period known as the Disney Renaissance. MGM Studios, now called Hollywood Studios, opens at Walt Disney World.

1991 • *Beauty and the Beast* is released. It's the first animated movie to be nominated for an Academy Award for Best Picture.

1992 • Euro Disney Resort, now called Disneyland Paris, opens.

1994 • *Beauty and the Beast* opens on Broadway. *The Lion King* is released.

1995 • *Toy Story* is released, the first Disney Pixar movie.

1996 • The Walt Disney Company acquires ABC.

1998 • Disney Cruise Line sets sail. Animal Kingdom opens at Walt Disney World.

2001 • Disney expands its line of DVDs to include the Gold Classic Collection and Platinum Collection with *Snow White and the Seven Dwarfs*. Disney California Adventure Park opens.

2003 • *Finding Nemo* and *Pirates of the Caribbean: The Curse of the Black Pearl* are released.

2004 • Michael Eisner is forced out as chairman of the board of directors and later resigns as CEO. Disney acquires the Muppets from the Jim Henson Company.

2005 • Bob Iger becomes Disney's next CEO. Iger divests several businesses that don't fit the Disney brand. Hong Kong Disneyland opens.

2006 • Disney acquires Pixar Animation Studios.

2009 • Disney acquires Marvel, creator of superheroes. Roy E. Disney dies.

2012 • Disney acquires Lucasfilm, maker of *Star Wars.*

2013 • *Frozen* is released and earns over $1.2 billion at the box office.

2014 • *Frozen* wins the Academy Award for Best Animated Feature Film.

2015 • *Big Hero 6* wins the Academy Award for Best Animated Feature Film. Disney's adjusted stock price hits $100 per share.

2016 • Disney has record sales. Shanghai Disney opens.

2018 • Disney employs approximately 200,000 cast members, including 1,700 Imagineers.

Source Notes

Chapter 2—Heading to Hollywood

page

9   *"I wanted Roy and I to be partners"*: Excerpts from the
     Walt Disney Family Museum website blog. "In Walt's
     Own Words: His Brother Roy." waltdisney.org/blog
     /walts-own-words-his-brother-roy. Accessed August
     25, 2017.

16   *Mickey Mouse became the first animated character to have
     a star:* Jennifer Fickley-Baker, "Fifteen Fun Facts for
     Mickey Mouse's Birthday," Walt Disney World Resort,
     Disney Parks blog, November 18, 2014. disneyparks.
     disney.go.com/blog/2014/11/happy-birthday-mickey
     -mouse-2.

Chapter 3—Mickey Mouse and Snow White

23   *among the top American film moneymakers of all time:*
     "All Time Box Office: Adjusted for Ticket Price
     Inflation," Box Office Mojo. www.boxofficemojo
     .com/alltime/adjusted.htm. Accessed July 17, 2017

Chapter 4—How Disney Went Public

26   *"Disney's initial public offering:* Nathan Buehler, "If You
     Had Invested Right After Disney's IPO," Investopedia,

December 1, 2015. www.investopedia.com/articles
/markets/120115/if-you-had-invested-right-after-disneys
-ipo.asp.

Chapter 8—One Hundred and One Improvements

59 *Walt Disney World was evacuated:* Frías, "40 Fun Facts
for Disney World's 40th Anniversary."

Chapter 9—Michael Eisner's Wild Ride

67 *Sales grew from $1.5 billion:* Eisner, "Bio." MichaelEisner
.com/bio. Accessed August 25, 2017.
cast members grew from 28,000 to 129,000: Holson,
"A Quiet Departure for Eisner at Disney."

Chapter 10—The Rescuers

72 *"clash of heritage versus innovation versus relevance":*
Siklos, "The Iger Difference."

77 *Disney acquired Lucasfilm:* Krantz, "Disney Buys Lucasfilm
for $4 Billion."

78 *the* Frozen *DVD became Amazon's best-selling children's
film:* Konnikova, "How 'Frozen' Took Over the World."

Bibliography

Barrier, Michael. *The Animated Man: A Life of Walt Disney.* Oakland: University of California Press, 2007.

Barrier, Michael. *Hollywood Cartoons: American Animation in Its Golden Age.* New York: Oxford University Press, 1999.

Eisner, Michael D. michaeleisner.com. Accessed July 17, 2017.

Encyclopedia of World Biography. "Michael Eisner Biography." www.notablebiographies.com/news/Ca-Ge/Eisner -Michael.html. Accessed July 17, 2017.

Frías, Carlos. "40 Fun Facts for Disney World's 40th Anniversary." *Palm Beach Post,* December 17, 2011.

Gallo, Carmine. "Customer Service the Disney Way." *Forbes,* April 14, 2011.

Holson, Laura M. "A Quiet Departure for Eisner at Disney." *New York Times,* September 26, 2005.

Konnikova, Maria. "How 'Frozen' Took Over the World." *New Yorker,* June 25, 2014.

Krantz, Matt, Mike Snider, Marco Della Cava, and Bryan Alexander. "Disney Buys Lucasfilm for $4 Billion." *USA Today,* October 30, 2012.

Pomerantz, Dorothy. "Five Lessons in Success from Disney's $40 Million CEO." *Forbes,* January 23, 2013.

Siklos, Richard. "The Iger Difference." *Fortune,* April 11, 2008.

Sim, Nick. "15 Things That Are Hidden Underground at Disney's Magic Kingdom." Theme Park Tourist, April 14, 2014. www.themeparktourist.com/features/201404 14/17536/15-things-are-hidden-underground-disneys -magic-kingdom.

Stewart, Whitney. *Who Was Walt Disney?* New York: Penguin Group, 2009.

Walt Disney Company. thewaltdisneycompany.com. Accessed July 17, 2017.

Walt Disney Company. *2016 Annual Report.* ditm-twdc-us .storage.googleapis.com/2016-Annual-Report.pdf.

Walt Disney Family Museum. waltdisney.org. Accessed July 17, 2017.

Walt Disney World News. "Walt Disney World Fun Facts." wdwnews.com/fact-sheets/2014/10/31/walt-disney-world -fun-facts. Accessed July 17, 2017.

Lowey Bundy Sichol is the author of
From an IDEA to . . . , the world's first business
biographies for kids. Lowey is also the founder of
Case Marketing, a specialized writing firm that
researches and composes case studies for business
schools and corporations. Her case studies have
been read by MBA students all over the world.
Lowey received a BA from Hamilton College and
an MBA from the Tuck School of Business at
Dartmouth College. She lives in Illinois with her
husband, Adam, three children, and two dogs who
look a little like Pluto and Goofy. Look for her
online at loweybundysichol.com.

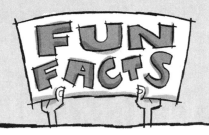

Lowey's favorite Disney characters are Huey, Dewey, and Louie, because they remind her of her three brothers.

FUN FACTS

Lowey's favorite ride at Walt Disney World is Splash Mountain.

If Lowey could have any Disney power, she would want Aladdin's magic carpet.

FROM AN IDEA TO NIKE

How Marketing Made Nike a Global Success

by LOWEY BUNDY SICHOL

illustrated by C. S. JENNINGS

FROM AN IDEA TO
GOOGLE

How Innovation at Google changed the world.

by **LOWEY BUNDY SICHOL**

illustrated by **C. S. JENNINGS**

FROM AN IDEA TO

LEGO

The Building Bricks Behind the World's Largest Toy Company

by **LOWEY BUNDY SICHOL**

illustrated by **C. S. JENNINGS**